Lyrics for Lucid Dreamers

Waltz till morning

Eric Dettelbach

Lyrics for Lucid Dreamers

Eric Dettelbach

ISBN: 1983899879
ISBN 13: 9781983899874
Library of Congress Control Number: 2018900757
CreateSpace Independent Publishing Platform
North Charleston, South Carolina

Dedication

———⨯⨯⨯———

Love

Special Thanks

THANK YOU TO LAURA ROBERTSON who assisted me by helping me gather and organize all the journals, notebooks, loose leaf pages, backs of flyers and paper towels on which this book was originally written. I can't express my thanks enough. Laura also provided her reflections, opinions and impressions which were insightful and helpful.

Morning Waltz to Night's Refrain

———∞∞∞———

Morning cool as quartz
smooth as lime
Fog lays low, drifts over roads.
Mirage waltzes across the green, song low and live
strumming' for the sky.
Hey it's me and I wonder
No sense in counting railroad ties till the day I die.

Jenny said pick me up
and we can groove all night.
Hawaiian halter top had me on lock.
She's a vision in that dress wrapped like a gift.
I hear the violins together and it's bliss.
She said "Can we ride" and I said "Get in".
Rode down to the flats in the 310
Banks of the Cuyahoga River.
Petals on the river float. Insects chatter.
Enter the night and watch you walk in the moonlight.
This summer's dream feels so open.
A sky train darts through space and light.
Take us anywhere we want to go.
I came back for you,
crossed states, miles.

Morning Waltz to Night's Refrain

Now it's time for the wind to roll cross your lips.
This night feels made for us.
We can walk forever.
Fire unsung

Muted Light

Echoes of Miles
"A star's a seed"
Picture me floating
an aura deemed

Scattered and clattered
the breaks do come,
I'm due for some

Distance game
Sprint

My sound is muted
This hydra life.

Goodbye September

Say goodbye September.
The wind it ushers out.
Shadows cloud the blood red moon
The shift in time, a sand grey beard
Strewn summer's names about like light.

Blurred spring, I remember still...
A scent, a smile, murals in the sand...
Flushed and breathless,
a wicked little laugh, soft rain in the dim street light,
the water's crest.
"Hush now" these sounds tap my soul.
Stored meditations.

Say goodbye September.
Sweetest July my love.
Mid August coda to June's refrain.
I reminisce on purple hues, smile in the sun,
in the moment, moving toward the valley.
Say goodbye September.
The wind chants in the night.
It blends with chimes,
this evening song of harvest moon,
an evil moon, October's entrance
swoons and Hallows eve dost loom.

Goodbye September

The energy, blood stirs…
leaves fall in wind and rain,
morning cool, sleeping weather.

Say goodbye September.
The light brings longer nights
and cover nape as chill may vindicate.

Say goodbye

Existence

Am I at the end
of an old phase?

Voices in the
head should be heeded
and are needed.
Do I live for self if selflessness the goal?

Time Twists like Sparrows Fly

no tears of sorrow has she felt
as loneliness has come and gone
for time it twists like sparrows fly
their ruby throats, no swallow sign

Tear in the Sun

Tear in the sun
find your way home
I feel your light
I see your face

A memory of what was not
Glazed tile walls
A walk in the past on truths that
pierced my globe

A different path
White light
The two are there playing together in a field

My thought is love
I love this thought
There are no forget-me-nots in this spectral vision
that glistens on temple

Tear in the sun
find your way home
I feel your light
I see your face

Fear River

Floating on Fear River
all up in the eddy

Mind lie

Fear River don't make sense
but still I float just the same

I lie awake
Fear River rambles over stones
Rattles me to the bone
Lives in shadows.

Fear River so cold and harsh.
It twists and burns with its twists and turns.
Channels deep and deadly
Like rain triggered memories.
I don't want to ride
I know it's wrong
but I do.
Soma driven half-wit
I can't stop.

Murals

Surrounded by Mother

These paintings left

Looking past the last times

She used to play tennis

Sitting by the court

So young

Just grass and clouds

Revert

Murals

Torn

All I think about is you
I know you think about me too
Even though there's no clear path for us,
I make these plans for us
I don't know quite what to do

Don't know if you feel the same
Our circumstance won't let me ask
or for that matter kiss your lips when we're alone,
so want to show you what I'm made of
You got a family I do too
I don't know quite what to do

It's because I think a time may come
When we're not across this isle
Maybe then we can find out
What will be or never be
My God! I just don't know

But forever and a day may come
Kicking it and laughing like we do
We may never get the chance to be
but I want you to know
Baby I love you

Torn

We may never get the chance to be
but I need to let you know
Baby I love you

But forever and a day may come
Kicking it and laughing like we do
We may never get the chance to be
but I want you to know
Baby I love you

We may never get the chance to be
but I need to let you know
Baby I love you
Baby I love you

Control

I'm strapped for you
But I can't stray

Never can kiss
Never can know

I'll just run my thoughts
like rivers over stone

All up in me
All across my mind

Conflict of dreams

Go for self or selflessness

Twisted connection (fate)

Want to... Will...Don't... Won't

See

I'm crazy for you

I Wish

I want to go to the show…with you

Pick you up at the parking
Then ride windows open

Lettn' us shine all the while
I'll be sippn' on you

Sip on wine
Turn the radio up
It's your favorite song
and I'm singing along

Stroll in the show
diggn' your vibe and
I'm sippin' on you

Dancing in the moonlight
Lettn' you shine bright
It's your favorite song
and I'm singing along

I Wish

End of summer dream and I'm sippn' on you
End of summer dream and I'm sippn' on you

I want to go to the show...with you

Love
  Support
    Growth
      Kindness
        Acts
Space
  Toughness
    Sex
      Loyalty
        Truth
Time
  Soul
    Body
      Head
        Treatise
Mind
  Heart
    Blood
      Breath
        Light

Meter Bleeds The Plain

On shattered knee

still tenacious a
and vibe out
with a limp
never simp though
That's the dif yo
Practice free throws
with my free flow
meter bleeds the plain
but its still the sam

16

The Good Side
of Purgatory

Sitting on the sidelines
watching the game safe and numb with chocolate

Bleed for more
Responsibility cock block
I fiend to assert
Don't wish for the pain, you just might get it...
fall off the edge

Fragile Psyche

Now you can see my poet's soul
See how hard I fall
You know I wish it wasn't
You know I wish I could keep it in
I cannot
And you're so sweet knowing how fragile

So what if the reason is my loss and my pain
So what if I'm flailing about out of control
I still feel what I feel
Maybe all of that internal just focuses me
Look, I know this goes nowhere but please indulge
to feel! To live! To love!

Bent Soul

My thoughts are out of control
Thinking about you and me
I'm playing out dates that will never be
I feel so absurd
I'm playing the fool again
I can't break free
I'll have to bend the key
Your light's a flash in the dark
and I still can't see
It's my burden now, I know this
I want so bad to talk with you but instead flow this

My agony to bear
My heart to ache
My soul to bend
My earth that shakes

My love to take
My love to make
My love to take away
To let my soul go free

A Love that's Pure

I've loved you from afar
for all these years

But now that you're leaving
you seem so near

I never pushed up on you
all those hours alone

But now that you're leaving
I'm sure I'll wonder when you're gone

Don't know if we'll talk much

It doesn't matter now

For a while our love was pure friendship

Didn't need no vows

I Lie to Myself

Please time come fast
break my love in half

I lie to myself
to make it through the day
I don't care what you won't say
I know you feel the same

Pretend were not in love
But our connection is too deep
I invent reasons not to like you
so it doesn't cut so deep

But when we talk
I can't fake how I feel
It's all over me
I can't be nothing but real

Been through all the "we can't do this"
Problem is I just can't turn things off
No matter what I know to be right

I Lie to Myself

So please time come fast
break my love in half
This feeling it breaks me
but I still want it to last
So please time come fast
break my love in half

Cause when I'm with you my heart still takes flight
Or because we're "only friends"
It sinks to the floor
For what can't be
I still truly adore
I know I can't have you
but I still want more

So please time come fast
break my love in half
This feeling it breaks me
but I still want it to last
So please time come fast
break my love in half

Your Smile

Your smile

turns me inside out

The way you tilt your head when we flirt

brings me so in

makes it hard to work

I always think you look cute even on bad hair days

I want to buy you those boots I know you're so into

I want so bad to stop

But I don't know how

Cause that smile keeps turning me out like the wild

Close in the Car

Thought control
Close in the car
Blood stirs
Race and blush
Snap out
Magnetic pull

(Journal)

The post work drive home was nauseating due to the rain, traffic and air pollution. I just need clean air and not to feel trapped! The Holidays always rev up the stress level. I will be taking some days off in the coming weeks to decompress and spend some time with family. I see a lot of ice skating in the near future.

Just you and the ice. Pushing, sliding. I love the emptiness. Rhythm and rhythm. No rhyme... Just now. I love the thick furs, hot coco. Lets go for a skate. Water on ice, so smooth. Smooth as a cliche. Smooth as a white tango. Gloves on, no fear. Free like giving a gift on Christmas. Free like doing the right thing.

Time Got Lost

Our time together
Is all to me
Never forget when you sang to me
Those brief moments when the outside world stops
Like eating Lotus flowers and time got lost

We Should Dance

I'm dancing by myself
when I could be dancing with you
Before that could ever happen there's a world of hurt
to go through
Probably couldn't even get to dance if I chose that path
But just the thought turns me out
I'm so dizzy I can't breath

Why am I pretending when I need to change my life?

Need to grab you by the hand and make a stand
Cause the time may be right
Both need something new in our life

The Moon and the Sea

Just you and I on our lunch hour
Went out to grab some soup
But never got inside the place
We just started listening and laughing
while the radio played
I told you how perfect we'd be in another life
Listened to Luke and Eric singing our life
You sang to me and looked in my eyes
I caught you looking even though you were acting shy
Nothing I like better then rapping to you
I'm feeling this moment like it's all to me
It made you happy too from what I could see
I'm just so in love like the moon and the sea

So Near Yet So Far

Man oh man
I'm in so deep
I want to stair in your eyes for eternity

Read you love poems
Alone in the car
You cried when I read them
So near yet so far

Told you I'd call you
Round 5:15
Called at 4:30 couldn't wait felt the need

And I can tell in your eyes
That it's me that you want
So true and caring
It's nobody's fault

We can talk all day
It not nearly enough
I'm not sure what I'd do if you called my bluff

So Near Yet So Far

Have to soul search
Till the early morn
I guess it's just like the stars
So near yet so far

Leaves in the Wind

We haven't talked in a while
So you're leaving my center
But still you sneak in
And I let you enter

Now just wondering
How you're doing and things
Hope all is well and just wondering

Thinking about your smile
and your laugh
My two favorite things
In my mind they last

Thinking about your love
and how it swept me aloft
Like leaves in the wind
On an autumn's day
That spin round and round
And then find their way

Now just wondering how you're doing and things
Hope all is well and just wondering
Thinking about your smile and just wondering

Kiss Your Tears

I know there are dark times and despair
Yes a world of hurt out here
We talk about how timing is everything
and how to make do
Without you I'm day by day
Wish it was me to kiss your tears away

Live Hard Love Hard

—❦—

I don't care what you got
I want to live hard love hard
Live hard
Love hard
Feel life

Pathways

The most painful love
A love that never comes to pass

An ill timed love in life, where pathways end like rivers
can't change course.

It haunts in visions that will never come
A planned first kiss on the steps in the rain
A holiday we cooked and laughed....all that laughter
and love.

The music and dance that never came

The things I showed and you showed me is all our life
will never be.

It's What You Call Making Beautiful Music Together

You and me on a ride in the country side
Rollin' down Old River Road
They were singing our song
We were singing along
and making up the parts we didn't know
We stopped in a park and went for a walk
To a spot up the hill you knew about
We talked about life
as we rested a while
then we walked back to the ride
Stepped the stones in the creek
Turned the radio up
and sang free like whatever…

It's what you call making beautiful music together

The Meta G's: Cleveland, Ohio Rock /
Hip Hop /Funk Fusion Group

⌘⌘⌘

Soft Chorus

Hold a rose, softly
as not to lilt
Violet view imbues
Each petal's glance
Each gaze a trance
Look upon this world
Pan's echo
Soft chorus rise and
call my name, I beg
I long for wind's whisper
and chimes sweet temperance

Love Song
(Rat Pack Style)

Come fly away with me
And call it destiny
You are my love you see
And it is time that holds us

Can't live without you girl
You are my Spring and Fall
And life's got good and bad
You're all I ever had

Our time is now to live
Don't get caught up and give

You are my angel light
I love to hold you tight

Don't run away from time
That's why I go for mine

And when the chips are down
That's when we all dig down

Chloe[1]

Chloe
I think about you constantly
Chloe
I think about you endlessly
Chloe

Won't you come home to me tonight
Won't you come home to me tonight
Won't you come home to me

Chloe
You're the girl of my dreams
Chloe
How I pray you're all right
Chloe
I think about you day and night
Chloe

Won't you come home to me tonight
Won't you come home to me tonight
Won't you come home to me

1 Written for my daughter when she was in the hospital. She was one pound ten ounces at birth.

Chloe

Chloe
You are the light that guides
Chloe
You are the sands of time
Chloe
You make me feel alive
Chloe

Won't you come home to me tonight
Won't you come home to me tonight
Won't you come home to me tonight
Won't you come home to me

Moments

Stillness
Seeing
Sound
Wind on face
Early morning fog lies on the grass
Sun peeks around the screen
Daughter playing quietly
Write
Connect
Calm my mind

Nature's Zeal

The most pleasant sound, the sound of song and music.
It wakens and heals.
Compels to move and be still.
No scribe can do justice,
No painting mirror, what to me is nature's zeal.

Just Thinking

All these thoughts like the night
Water drips down pipes to the tune
I wonder at the smallness of my place… outside
any world…our world

Maybe she was right how she went through life

Seemingly in-control persona fades to blurry frailty
etched and tethered all the while rippling with time

See You

Through the crevice
I see you, your soul good and true
and caring.

Working Man

I wake up early in the morning
The birds are my alarm

I wake up early in the morning
said the birds are my alarm

My wife may be up too,
makes the coffee in the morn

You know I got to get
ready for work, kiss my baby,
that's the way of the world

You know I got to get
ready for work, kiss my baby,
that's the way of the world

You know I do my best to keep above water
To ball you gotta fall

You know I do my best to keep above water
To ball you gotta fall

Fickle Death

No triumph in sorrow
Montage of pain
Call in the night…
I mean phone rings.
"So that's that," of the end.

My own heart heavy

This I feel
Oh fickle death when near
my brow is furled, my mind
is busy, blood is hot.

No thoughts of why, fickle death.
Discrimination all inclusive.
This man I know a solid soul.
That I respect.

Eyes closed but awake
Strain to move
I know this feeling from a dream.
The dream where you struggle to
scream, but nothing…
The dream where you want
to run but can't move.

Fickle Death

Exert to open eyes…last breath
Then rest.
You're flying now…
Coming in low over the lake.[1]
White caps crisp on the water's crest

Shooting back up in the clouds now.
You're vertical, going higher and
higher… you're free. To freedom's gate.

1 My man was a pilot who said he liked to come in low over the lake even
though he wasn't supposed to.

Gravity

Pangs that I resist
lest I fall back
as time bends

Tantalus longed to feed
on grapes and what
gluttony would bide, if only
within reach.

No measure to stem
the tide that Pan's
fountain rains.

Gravity, I lose control
Buried desire

Swimming in vertigo…
breathless.
Hands warm, heart beat brisk.

Angels and Devils do
battle on the music of my
mind.

What is Not

———— ∞∞∞ ————

So what of the future? Just keep working.
Fight through the melee, the hullabaloo.
We are all concerned for one reason or another.

Balance
        Past
                Present
                        Future

You can't trip on what may never come to pass. You
can't live your life, dream your dreams, plan a future
based on what you don't have.

Cranberry Streetfest

Close eyes
Face the sun
Bring it down, way down
Intimate
Quiet
We got respect
That's important to me
Respect the craft

THE HAX

Look Before U Leap

You've got to look
before you leap

Step round the circle
Tread on light feet
Don't make a creak

Don't let them hear
you approach

Survey through the trees like a scout

Hide in the margin

like October to snow

Scattered on fringe

No need to lunge in

Even though I creep
Still walk on beat

You've got to look
before you leap

Rescue

You're so scared in that corner, face up against the wall.

I know you've been out on streets, surviving, living in shadows, swimming in fear, so quiet, shaking in the dark.

You've been searching.

Now you've been led here.

You can't trust it, but it's real, this love.

You've never felt before.

Don't quite know how to act.

It will take some time, but
I can see you quiver less.

You can't show love yet, but
I can see it's in your heart.

This is your home now.

Rescue

You've finally come home.

I need you to understand.

You're home, no need to fear.

Don't fear in your heart.

Stay On Point

Sometimes you just have to take it.

There are those that will treat you poorly, unfairly. This is life. Our reaction to these circumstances is definition.

Some battle in the mind and replay the anger. Some engage in the moment, returning serve with centrifugal force. Others channel into so called positive energy. Oft we let the wrath of vindictiveness eat us. Feel the pain of love. Redirect and think of smoothing and working wood and gardens. Feel the summer breeze and smell the soft rain. No stagnation suffocation.

I need to get to the point... where depression parts and light rains warm. Realize this feeling is fleeting, as our emotions are many. And be OK with the sharpness and limits. Control meditations of mind and heart... like...

Accept falling short without conceding.
Perfection through discipline like Monk's calligraphy.

Remember

Rag-time shoots soul to the air
There's a spicy young woman
in a cool yellow sundress
her hair in the wind

To the sun
Remember the ocean?
The salty fragrance that whispered away
Painting murals in the sand nobody saw cause the tide
quickly washed them away.
Remember the heat in the city?
Sitting on the pavement taking in all the madness like
Simon in New York City.
Remember the Court Jester?
Walking the streets with ten to twenty.
Remember the soft rain in the street lights?
How jazzed we felt watching the night
Only happens once in a lifetime.
Remember the night at the warehouse?
You wore that sexy Asian dress,
Chris and Kurt kissed wild,
Babylon sister praying for priests.

Remember

Remember laughing chance at 3:00 am?
Billie's tape and starry eyes blazing a path right in me
like southern blues,
Red wine writings and kitchen table poems…
Still read them
Beyond the streets as wide and bright as the night
Like you

Light Rhyme Scheme

So much to do, so at times overwhelmed,
when I truly reflect, I'm either going or flowing.
See I never hesitated to try and make things right.
It's the sign of the times and you know that I'm light.

There are fears when you put yourself out to get play.
It's the truth that I kick and the rhyme I display.
Sync the player, connect and check out, no doubt.
Leave the stress
Don't worry,
Livewire and out.

Rip U

Don't come at me like that
'cause I'll break you in half
Held my tongue
'cause I'm nice
Think twice
put you on ice
with a verbal assault.
See you fronted
and as it resulted
you were stunted.
Came abrupt, you didn't see
left you with jaw open,
I'll have you thinking back
years from now on this moment,
teachable moment
better own it
Try to vic it
meaning pilfer.
What's mine remains cipher,
the interconnection the ignition that lights you.
Start a fire in the mire
Plains fields and all the like
Of that ilk

Rip U

Maintain
And that blood that stains,
likes bars on the mind,
so unkind with disdain.

CHECKER

1. RUNAWAY
2. PLANET OF ANTS
3. AIN'T NOTHING
4. THIRD REALM
5. BLITZKRIEG

Checker band photo circa 1998

There's a Love
to Guide Us

This thing I remember
from 1,000 years ago

Seems it will never die

Same old phrases, different faces
on the Sunday morning shows

She turns it off
looks at the sky

I know there is a light
to guide us home

More brilliant than the sun

I know there is a love
to guide us on

Stand in it unsung

There's a Love to Guide Us

Factor wars on graphs
to see the trends

Another one's around the bend

The "War on Terror" has no end
by virtue of its name

The machine doesn't
have an end game

And some waste time
on the blame game

for all their past woes

I say don't get caught up
look up and look around

And just let it flow

There's a Love to Guide Us

I know there is a light
to guide us home

More brilliant than the sun

I know there is a love
to guide us on

Stand in it unsung

So each morning
I can look in your eyes
I thank my lucky stars
Because this turning world
is so much to handle

I crave a simple life…
Alive with song
A symphony of one
that will not end

There's a Love to Guide Us

A rain that melts the snow
The sun it dries the rain
and we begin again

I know there is a light
to guide us home

More brilliant than the sun

I know there is a love
to guide us home

Stand in it unsung

Maginot Lines

———— ⚮ ————

This warm December wind has me feeling so off. Just doesn't make sense to me. Beneficial light has many crossed up. Take advantage of what you got. Meaning spend time with those you love.

As time passes, vice has no place? Closer to death, no time to waste. Does vice portend life? Where memories are made. That chocolate cake. That night "We drank til morning and watched the sun rise." A payoff, or only regret and tragedy as twist of fate percentage grows when vice does flow.

"Nothing good happens when you're out at 2:00 am."

Then there are those who try so hard a pious life to lead, yet tragic circumstance befall. My heartaches… and I listen to a friend whose life has twisted. I contemplate the worry and regret and pray the pain relieves and submerges 'till morrow's pain elucidates.

Life's arbitrary. No karma burns as good die young and "devil's" wealth and debauchery may provide a halo for some time. And when life strikes, are they

Maginot Lines

"getting theirs?" or is it only life's tragic blend? Or is
the hunt so deep that armor has harmed? The armor
that protects us all in some form or another. We ratio-
nalize, debate and reason. We "don't care" anymore
and yet we all can break again and again.

Cudell Park

Threshold for pain
equals threshold for change
and when it all rolls through
freight train through the rain.
Stains washed away (never washed)
the footprints in the grass and snow
through the field of Cudell Park.

I wish I could roll back ticks.
Space and lace (the time continuum)
Freedom earned
And re-upped! Lose fraction or
percent if tongue is held.
The Invisible Man or in this
case The Invisible Boy.
Never looked at face.
Never looked in eyes.

Checker

Tamir

Never forget Cleveland... World

Cudell Park

Couldn't have looked in eyes

Invisible boy

Timeless Ellison

Rippled pain

Fear's echo heard round world

One chance is another death

All World Tamir

Smile, a Weapon Against Cancer

—— ∞∞∞ ——

Let go into emptiness
this cancer…
The smile is a weapon.
It lightens my spirit when
all appears lost.

Keep smiling, don't forget now…
adrift in oceans and sundrops.
Hands full of soil, washed over
Let go of the fear
There is solace in
the minuteness
the namelessness.
Blip in the construct
Stay healthy
I'm away with dance
Healing dance, you make me smile
My alchemy

Want To Hang?

You want to hang with me?
You want to sing with me?

I think you know what time
it is so won't you give it to me
all the blue notes I desire
My mood is sentimental
I go long on the "L"
There is no need for reluctance
Give you all I got
Didn't try for not
Turned the key to the lock

Blue note got me
Melancholy twang
So tell me now, do you want to hang?

You want to hang with me?
You want to sing with me?

Rock This Joint

She works a nine to five
Stays late, gets out, what she do
She got a few kids too

So sexy, stuff she does bothers him
She gets bothered too
Hits that whisky bottle on the way in

Still takes pleasure in the little things.

She got sidetracked and gut wrenched
That hurdled pace so up in your face

She wonder why and this and that
Don't sweat it sweet lady
We all live life
Try to stay on point
"Rock this funky joint" [1]

1   Poor Righteous Teachers

Family in One

you've come a long way in the last year

i'm so glad you found our home

with that kind of base you can extend

with that base you can even defend

you've got to get that steel spine

intertwined with light

got to keep the wall strong

but at the same time break it down

and keep pushin' on

and don't forget to look around

I Can't Help

Triggers awaken pain
Try to catch breath
Shivering
Mind switched
I'm here to help
Let go of the pain

Let it out
Let yourself be free!

Driving Music

I want to spend time with you.

Even if that means sitting by your side while you
engage in another pursuit

being still and silent...

or

I can be engaged with
something else as well, as we sit.

Presence without intrusion...like driving music

Juke Joint Filthy

Sweaty mess

Head so clear

Love that dance

Stirs me still

Heart pulse, lick lips, shake hips that rumble

Whole place on swoll, rain wet and tumble

Curves on that

Grip on fat

You like it like that

Cut real low

That is the tempo

Off in the cut

Juke Joint Filthy

Close in the shadows

Eyes rolled back

You look so vexed

so on beat

so on sex

Juke joint filthy

They Laugh at Us

Lying
Denying
We just keep on buying
Schizoid
Devil Toy
They just keep on trying
Beat 'em
Take 'em down
Kick it for the street
Point blank range
It's the emblem for defeat

And yo how they like to laugh
You turn around and they stab your back

Do this
Freak it
Back Breaker
Tweak this
All you've got to do is ask
And they can't compete with

They Laugh at Us

Finesse it
Bless it
Take it to that level
Title take sound
With the bass and all that treble

And oh I never kick the half
And yo all you got to do is ask

Trade it
Save it
Put it on the shelf
What the fuck for
Make you think
about what's left

Travesty
Innocence
Lost in the abyss
In the chasm
The great tavern
And it's all gone amiss

They Laugh at Us

Run amok
What the fuck
Let it bleed
Until they're blue
I'm so sick of the line
Spin machine
And they knew

And yo how they
Like to laugh
You turn around
And they stab your back

And Oh
I never kick the half
And yo all you've got to do is ask

What

What if I could take you on a ride
All laid back tall with brown eyes
What if I could be the one and only
What if time stood still
What if we could chill
What if we could break it down
'til the early light.
What if we could take flight
Just imagine that
Time to relax taking it easy on a hazy day and making
you sway
It's like lemon drop sunshine
A beautiful memory
What if we could rewind time would u lend me some
for fun or just giggles and laughs
What if I wanted to get silly girl
Would u laugh

What

What if my mind played tricks on me
Would I get through it or would I just be
crazy insane through life who would notice!
What if my password was Lotus

What

Drunk like Otis at times
Feel the rhymes
What if my madness
got turned into gladness
insanity crept out cold
What if a relative game got old
What if I was cold
What if this mission I employ turn tables
and spun fables
The sequence cold money bold situational breakdown
You know that I'm Diggy
Because I kick it however you want me to
Accommodational puncture wound
To consume the room
In the temple of doom
I never ever Frontin'
No matter who's in the room

What

Boom Baby
Boom Boom Boom Bap
Snare on the drums
With the rat tat tat tat
So get to that baby
'cause you know that's the haps

Musical demography
Analyze our democracy
Searching for what
My flow constantly
So here we go
you know it's me

What

Running Out of Time

You're running out of time
That's why I go for mine
Don't want to lose control
You're know you're getting old

I don't know
But I've been told
You play the cards you're dealt
And you don't never fold

You're running out of time
Your luck is on the dime
You got a pinpoint plan
This is the last stand

I don't know
But I've been told
You play the cards you're dealt
And you don't never fold

You're running out of time
Don't even take a glance
Cause this is your last chance
You got to keep that stance

Running Out of Time

The clock goes tick-tick-tick
You can't be done with it
I know you just said so
And know it's time to go
You got a nervous twitch
Don't be a son of a bitch

Running Out of Time

They'll try to slow you down
And they'll be leaching on
Don't be looking back
You got to stay on track

You're running out of time
I think you know what I mean
Don't ever lose the game
And keep that card up your sleeve

I don't know
But I've been told
You play the cards you're dealt
And you don't never fold

You got a nervous twitch
Don't be a son of a bitch

You're running out of time
Your luck is on the dime
You got a pinpoint plan
This is the last stand

Drifting up River

I called you
up in Philly
the other day

You sounded so good
But I'm across states
trying to make my stake

Guess the time's
passing by on this drifting schooner
If I could just grab a hold I could make it there sooner
Nothing I'd like better pick you up in my cruiser
But I let you fly…and keep asking why.

You wore that halter top
That had me non stop
So fine on my mind
We just laughed and played
Wore your hair that way

Drifting up River

But for now I'm floating up river
on this drifting schooner
If I could just grab a hold I could make it there sooner
Nothing I'd like better than pick you up in my cruiser
But I let you fly…and keep asking why.

I'll Cry a Thousand Tears for Love

I lay in bed waiting for her
I want her to love me like she did

Am I a fool to pursue this dream
'cause time collapses us like a vice
It scams
I must cut her loose again and feel the sorrow
Break those border lines being built for tomorrow
I know fear I see perceptively
Cut right through to the truth
She knows so well what to do
Just take time
I know that is the answer

I blame winds' songs
don't know the progression
In fact how often does
it break the session
But still love conquers for me
Never learn my lesson

I'll Cry a Thousand
Tears for Love

The path is clanking and still cuts all the trends
So personal leaving little notes
and when I feel her touch that's all she wrote
I rush to lose my cool which I never want to
Try to put in check but I just can't stop

I guess it's true what they say
the heart wants what it wants
for to feel that touch, a forget-me-not
I won't cry again for love I pray
'cause that pain never really does stay away.

I listen for the car to pull up...park
The door shut she crawls in and it all just starts

Burn Down Purple Sunrise

Sun inside your mind
burns bright through sun and rain

So burn down purple sunrise
my blood pumps red as day.

A sea of bodies roll
A flag shines from within
Stand at ease little one
The nighttime comes
The tide's gonna roll away

So burn down purple sunrise
my blood pumps red as day.

Light your smoke
Sit back on high
Remember your sweet lady the way she sighed
A smooth stone in a brook that rambles through time

Burn Down Purple Sunrise

So burn down purple sunrise
my blood pumps red as day.

The sun inside your mind
can blind itself one day
So burn down purple sunrise
my blood pumps red as day

A sea of bodies roll
A flag shines bright within
A star at ease through ocean tide
A shade bold as sun

So burn down purple sunrise
my blood pumps red as day.

Washed Over

Sitting out on the front porch
Candle waves in the moonlight
Cars careen and sirens scream
in the distant night
I hear laughter down the street
beckon my blues away
and I finally feel empty, washed over again

Miss Keys is singing to the other balladeers
and the kids cross the street
get rowdy and say, "I ain't going that way,"
c'mon let's go back"
so Scotty walks that way

And the crickets sing their love songs
and I want you even more
than the first day we met when I was riding downtown
And the neighbor shouts "Daisy come here"
as the dog runs away
and people's life changed in an instant on that day

And I finally feel empty washed over again.

Washed Over

Elsie never looked back
when she walked out the door
There really wasn't nothing' left for her
back there anymore
So she freed herself of all that pain
All she could hear was the sound of rain

And she finally felt empty
washed over again and again
And I finally feel empty washed over again

ABOUT THE AUTHOR

⸺⸺

A NATIVE OF LAKEWOOD, OHIO, Eric Dettelbach studied writ-
ing and poetry at Ohio University. He has performed across
the country in the course of his musical career and has found-
ed acts such as The Meta Gs, Checker, Diggy, Pleasuredome
Entertainment, and The Hax. Along with Bruce Jackson, he
heralded the original fusion wave of live instrumentation with
hip-hop in the Cleveland music scene and assimilated the
rhythms you can hear echoed in his poetry today.

Made in the USA
Lexington, KY
30 November 2018